When FAITH Meets the
IMPOSSIBLE

Gerald R. Nash

The believer's faith in God enables
the Lord to do miraculous things for
him and through him.

Pacific Press Publishing Association
Mountain View, California
Oshawa, Ontario

Library of Congress Cataloging in Publication Data
Nash, Gerald R
  When faith meets the impossible.

  1. Faith. 2. Nash, Gerald R. II. Title.
BV4637.N37   234'.2   80-24758
ISBN 0-8163-0404-1

Preface

In this booklet we are not attempting to cover all aspects of faith. We are endeavoring to emphasize that phase of faith that enables one to have confidence in God's promises. The kind of faith that "looks beyond the difficulties, and lays hold of the unseen, even Omnipotence, therefore, it cannot be baffled."—*Gospel Workers*, p. 262.

There is danger when we relate our own experiences to show what great things the Lord has done that some may misunderstand and think we are proud of our personal accomplishments. God forbid. I want to make it perfectly clear that in the experiences I relate I take no credit to myself. I was only the instrument. It was the power of God, and to Him be all the praise and honor and glory.

"The Saviour's promise [John 14:12] to His disciples is a promise to His church to the end of time. God did not design that His wonderful plan to redeem men should achieve only insignificant results. All who will go to work, trusting not in what they themselves can do, but in what God can do for and through them, will certainly realize the fulfillment of His promise."—*The Desire of Ages*, p. 667.

When Faith Meets the Impossible is sent forth with an earnest prayer that its message may be used of God to deepen that personal faith which works by love and to impart courage and inspiration to "attempt great things for God" and to "expect great things from God."

The author

Contents

Faith and How It Works

Faith is belief, but it is more. Faith is trust, but it is even more. Faith is a living power. Faith takes God at His word, and acts. Faith overcomes difficulties that seem altogether impossible. Faith wins victories over enemies that seem fortified behind impregnable walls.

When one takes hold of a promise of God and works in harmony with the conditions given in His Word for claiming that promise, then it makes no difference how huge the challenge or how impossible it seems. We must believe the promise and work accordingly. Faith without action is dead. Faith knows no obstacle and listens to no opposition from the evil one. Faith never stops to look at circumstances or to ponder results. Faith looks only to God. "Genuine faith has its foundation in the promises and provisions of the Scriptures."—*Gospel Workers*, p. 260.

Jesus told His disciples, "If ye have faith . . . , nothing shall be impossible." Faith, says the *Seventh-day Adventist Dictionary*, is "a confidence of heart and mind in God and His ways that leads one to act in accordance with His sovereign will." Hebrews 11:1 in *Today's English Version* reads: "To have faith is to be sure of the things we hope for, to be certain of the things we cannot see." The thought is here expressed that faith is a confidence which we have toward God and all that pertains to Him. "He that cometh to God must believe that he is." Hebrews 11:6. God has chosen faith as the road that we must travel if we are to please Him.

Jesus gives us a formula for success. He said, "Have faith in God. For verily I say unto you, That whosoever shall say unto this mountain, Be thou removed, and be thou cast into the sea; and shall not doubt in his heart, but shall believe that those things which he saith shall come to pass; he shall have whatsoever he saith." Mark 11:22, 23.

Look at that formula. "Faith in God," not in ourselves—but in God. "For verily"—He emphasizes the fact that what He has to say may be hard to believe, but it is the truth. "Whosoever"—that means any person. It means you; it means me. "Say unto this mountain"—that is specific and definite. Select any circumstance of your own life that is standing in your way, and this formula will apply. "Be thou removed"—taken out of my way. No longer can it hurt me. "Cast into the sea"—gone forever. "Shall not doubt . . . but shall believe"—it is through faith in God's promises that victory is achieved.

What a wonderful promise! This promise is unlimited, except for the limits we ourselves place on it because of our inability to accept God's statement.

"Faith is an essential element of prevailing prayer. . . . With the persevering faith of Jacob, with the unyielding persistence of Elijah, we may presnt our petitions to the Father, claiming all that He has promised."—*Prophets and Kings*, pp. 157, 158.

Jesus did not intend that His disciples go around removing mountains. His miracles were not of this nature. He was trying to convey the fact that in doing God's work nothing is impossible if one has faith.

"Though the grain of mustard seed is so small, it contains that same mysterious life principle which produces growth in the loftiest tree. When the mustard seed is cast into the ground, the tiny germ lays hold on every element that God has provided for its nutriment, and it speedily develops a sturdy growth. If you have faith like this, you will lay hold upon God's word, and upon all the helpful agencies He has appointed. Thus your faith will strengthen, and will bring to your aid the power of heaven. The obstacles that are piled by Satan across your path, though apparently as insurmountable as the eternal hills, shall disappear before the demand of faith. 'Nothing shall be impossible unto you.' "—*The Desire of Ages,* p. 431.

"Faith cometh by hearing, and hearing by the word of God," the Bible says. Faith comes to us by hearing—by listening attentively to and heeding the Word of God. This is the meaning of Paul's explanation of the source of faith. God not only gives every man some faith with which to start life, but He also gives something for faith to work upon to make it grow—His Holy Word. And as we believe, our faith grows and becomes active, living—a fruit-bearing faith.

Faith—strong, courageous faith—starts the mind to planning ways and means of reaching the goal we have set. Faith in God is the only known assurance against failure. The moment you have genuine faith in God's promises, success is assured.

"When we give ourselves wholly to God and in our work follow His directions, He makes Himself responsible for its accomplishment. He would not have us conjecture as to the success of our honest endeavors. Not once should we even think of failure. We are to co-operate with One who knows no failure."—*Christ's Object Lessons,* p. 363.

In *Gospel Workers,* page 19, we find this sentence: "Workers for Christ are never to think, much less speak of failure in their work." When we surrender our lives to Him, God makes Himself responsible for our success.

We must never stop reaching out in faith for larger and ever larger accomplishments. Some are allowing themselves to become Christian dwarfs as far as faith is concerned. Reaching and yearning does not imply withdrawing or making excuses. We must believe and have full confidence in God's promises and leadings. The degree of our success depends entirely on the strength of our belief. Seldom does one accomplish more than he sets out to accomplish. It is our thinking, our attitude, that really counts. It is impossible to separate faith from victory. It has been said, "All His biddings are enablings." We must remember that we are laborers together with God.

It is a part of God's plan to grant us, in answer to the prayer of faith, that which He would not bestow did we not ask. "The greatest victories gained for the cause of God are not the result of labored argument, ample facilities, wide influence, or abundance of means; they are gained in the audience chamber with God, when with earnest, agonizing faith men lay hold upon the mighty arm of power.

"True faith and true prayer—how strong they are! . . . Faith is trusting in God,—believing that He loves us, and knows what is for our best good."—*Gospel Workers,* p. 259.

"Why should the sons and daughters of God be reluctant to pray, when prayer is the key in the hand of faith to unlock heaven's storehouse, where are treasured the boundless resources of Omnipotence?"—*Steps to Christ*, pp. 94, 95.

The prayer of faith is not a blindly selfish demand that whatever we want must be given to us without regard for the rights or needs of others. Prayer unites our will to God's will and helps us to understand what His will is for us. The faith required for a positive answer to prayer is the faith that causes us to trust Him, asking only for those things that are in accord with His will.

This trust produces in us perfect confidence that God will give us what we ask for, since our request is according to His will. We read in 1 John 5:14, 15, RSV: "And this is the confidence which we have in him, that if we ask anything according to his will He hears us. And if we know that he hears us in whatever we ask, we know that we have obtained the requests made of him."

God always hears and answers sincere prayers. Sometimes He says Yes, granting our requests. Sometimes He says Wait, because He can see the end from the beginning and knows what is best for us. Sometimes He says No.

He said No to Moses because his request was not in harmony with God's plan. Moses wrote: "I besought the Lord at that time, saying, 'O Lord God, thou hast begun to shew thy servant thy greatness, and thy mighty hand: for what God is there in heaven or in earth, that can do according to thy works, and according to thy might? I pray thee, let me go over, and see the good land that is beyond Jordan, that goodly mountain, and Lebanon. But the Lord was wroth with me for your sakes, and would not hear me: and the Lord said unto me, Let it suffice thee; speak no more unto me of this matter. Get thee up into the top of Pisgah, and lift up thine eyes westward, and northward, and southward, and eastward, and behold it with thine eyes: for thou shalt not go over this Jordan. But charge Joshua, and encourage him, and strengthen him: for he shall go over before this people, and he shall cause them to inherit the land which thou shalt see." Deuteronomy 3:23-28.

God also said No to Paul, who suffered from a "thorn in the flesh." He writes, "For this thing I besought the Lord thrice, that it might depart from me. And he said unto me, My grace is sufficient for thee: for my strength is made perfect in weakness. Most gladly therefore will I rather glory in my infirmities, that the power of Christ may rest upon me. Therefore I take pleasure in infirmities, in reproaches, in necessities, in persecutions, in distresses for Christ's sake: for when I am weak, then am I strong." 2 Corinthians 12:8-10.

God's Miraculous Leadings

How can faith achieve victory? Let me relate a few personal experiences emphasizing the fact that when one gets his thinking straight and places his confidence and faith in God's promises and power, the size of the undertaking does not matter, providing the request is in harmony with His will.

In 1927 Mrs. Nash and I went to Africa as missionaries. We arrived at Malamulo Mission in Nyasaland, now called Malawi, which was to be our home and where I was to be in charge of the Training Institute. Each year during the time of the union committee meeting the brethren discussed ways and means of entering new territory.

During the first few years at the mission I became very much aware of the need to establish our work in Zomba, the former capital of Nyasaland. At the time we were in Africa, Nyasaland was a British protectorate, though it has since become independent.

Zomba lies about seventy miles south of Lake Nyasa. It is the center of a tobacco- and cotton-raising region. Many beautiful government homes nestled on the mountainside. But we had no mission work in that area. Year after year I felt more and more impressed that we should begin mission work in that area.

In 1932 during the union committee session the brethren were once more discussing the establishment of new mission outposts. I made an earnest appeal for the Zomba area.

Imagine my surprise when the union president turned to me and said, "Brother Nash, I feel you are the man for the task."

Without hesitation the brethren voted that I take three month's leave of absence from my regular work and go to Zomba for the purpose of opening new work there. A fellow missionary, two leading African pastors, and two young teachers were assigned to work with me.

We packed our Chevrolet truck with food and everything we would need for the trip. Our location for the effort was about sixteen miles from the city; so we could get to town for supplies now and then. The site for our camp was on high ground, and several large trees afforded us shade.

The people in that area belonged to the Yao tribe and were mostly of the Moslem faith. Therefore we knew we would have to work hard and spend much time in prayer, claiming God's promises. Our efforts seemed worthless. The adults would not attend the meetings. The children came, and we taught them songs and told them Bible stories.

At the end of three months we had not a single convert. In fact, we did not even have one good interest.

Back at Malamulo Mission the people asked us for a report of our three-month effort. We had no report to give. Nevertheless, I kept praying for the people of the Zomba area.

At the next annual meeting once more the opening of new work was discussed. No one mentioned the Zomba area. At last I stood up and pleaded with the brethren to remember that area.

The union president said, "Surely you would not want to go back there after your experience last year."

My reply was, "I never wanted to do anything so much in my life." I added that I had started something that I felt I must finish. Then I quoted: " 'If we have the interest that John Knox had when he pleaded before God for Scotland, we shall have success. He cried, "Give me Scotland, Lord, or I die." And when we take hold of the work and wrestle with God, saying, "I must have souls; I will never give up the struggle," we shall find that God will look upon our efforts with favor.' "—*Evangelism,* p. 294.

Once more the brethren assigned the task of opening up mission work in the Zomba area to me. I took with me an African pastor and a young teacher.

"This is it," the brethren said. "We cannot invest so much in an area where we do not get results. There are too many other openings."

Earnestly the pastor, the teacher, and I prayed and worked. This time many people attended the meetings, old and young alike. We could hardly keep up with the interests. God worked in a miraculous way. At the end of the summer we had 160 converts. How could we leave these dear people?

We couldn't leave our translator to do the follow-up work since he was one of our main staff members at the Malamulo Training School. We had no one that could be spared who knew the local dialect. What should we do?

We joined with the workers at Malamulo Mission and prayed about the situation.

A few days later an intelligent-looking young man came into my office at the mission and handed me a letter from Elder S. G. Maxwell, then superintendent of the East African Union Mission. It read as follows:

"This letter is being given you by one of our recent graduates from our Training School here in Kenya. His name is Jim Malowa. He is an outstanding young man. We wanted him to stay and work for us, but he wants to go to his home village and work for his own people. If you can use him, well and good; if not, please see that he comes back to us."

We learned that Jim came from one of the villages where we now had the most interests.

"Do you speak the local language?" I asked.

"Ah, bwana," he replied, "that is my mother tongue."

Jim told us he had left Nyasaland to look for work, as so many others did, and had wandered over into Kenya. While there, he had met some of our believers. After a time he had joined a Bible class and then entered the training school there and became a baptized member of the church. Upon completing the course he asked for a letter of introduction to the principal of the Malamulo Training Institute.

Immediately we saw that God had led in this situation. He had a trained leader ready at the proper time. Our faith had been honored.

Jim went to the Zomba area. After being there a few months he called for help. Elder F. L. Chapman, who had charge of the South Nyasaland Field at the time, answered the call. Shortly after Elder Chapman went to Zomba, a call came for more help. Elder M. M. Webster and I both responded.

As a result of Jim's work and the work of a faithful colporteur, named Division, who had been successful in selling a number of books in the area, the work grew rapidly.

Soon a school was needed. However the District Commissioner turned down our request for a permit. He said that too many churches, especially one teaching that the seventh day was the Sabbath, would confuse the minds of the local people.

But God had His plans for that area.

Six hundred miles to the north of Zomba, near the Luwazi Mission, the wife of the Provincial Commissioner for the northern half of Nyasaland, now Malawi, became critically ill. There was no doctor in miles. But as God would have it, Elder Lyndon Tarr, superintendent of the Luwazi Mission, came along on his motorcycle one morning and met the Provincial Commissioner near his home. The two men stopped to chat. The commissioner soon shared the news of his wife's serious illness and his feeling of despair.

"My wife is a trained nurse," Elder Tarr spoke up. "Perhaps she might be able to help your wife."

The commissioner suggested that Elder Tarr take his car and go back to the mission and get Mrs. Tarr.

When the Tarrs arrived at the commissioner's home, Mrs. Tarr went immediately to see what she could do for the patient. A few minutes later she told her husband that unless God took over, the woman would die.

Elder Tarr called Mr. Anderson, the commissioner, and explained the situation to him. He then invited the man to join him and his wife in prayer.

Fervently Elder and Mrs. Tarr prayed that God would restore Mrs. Anderson to health. After prayer Mrs. Tarr checked the patient's pulse. At first there seemed very slight improvement. Mrs. Tarr stayed for several days. Gradually the fever subsided, the patient's pulse became stronger. God blessed the efforts of Mrs. Tarr, and at last Mrs. Anderson was out of danger.

The commissioner felt deeply grateful for the help his wife had received, and he asked if there was anything he could do to help our mission work.

Soon after this experience Mr. Anderson was transfered to the southern part of the territory. He was to be the Provincial Commissioner, with headquarters in Blantyre, a city not far from Zomba.

Elder H. M. Sparrow, the union superintendent, and I requested an interview with Mr. Anderson soon after his arrival in Blantyre. We made a plea for the permit to establish schools in the Zomba area.

Mr. Anderson told us that he expected the District Commissioner from Zomba that very morning. He promised to talk to us later.

No one knows what Mr. Anderson said to the District Commissioner or the commissioner to him. However, within five days we received a letter from the District Commissioner which read as follows: "Further to my letter of the 20th ult. [last month] with reference to your application for schools in the Zomba district. This is to inform you that I have recently visited the three places where you are requesting permission to establish schools, and after having reconsidered the matter, I have decided that I will place the applications before the Committee with the recommendation that they be approved."

Truly and quietly the Spirit of the great God of heaven had been doing His work. Let us briefly follow the steps. A young man, guided to another country, came in contact with Seventh-day Adventists. Their influence led him to join the church and to enter one of our schools. Upon graduation he determined to go back home and take the message to his people. He arrived in his homeland just when he was most needed. Then, when it seemed impossible to establish schools, again God worked for us. An influential woman became ill. Elder Tarr and the woman's husband, the Provincial Commissioner, met on the road. Elder Tarr brought his wife to nurse the sick woman. The government moved the Provincial Commissioner and his wife to the south, where the Adventists had requested permission to build schools and had been denied.

Do things usually just happen as they did in this story? The answer is obvious. There had to be an unseen guiding power.

Such manifestations of the movings of the Spirit of God give us courage. Surely the promise of the Lord is being fulfilled: " 'Thou wilt keep him in perfect peace, whose mind is stayed on Thee: because he trusteth in Thee.' The arm of Omnipotence is outstretched to lead us onward and still onward. Go forward, the Lord says; I will send you help. It is for My name's glory that you ask; and you shall receive. Those who are watching for your failure shall yet see My word triumph gloriously. 'All things, whatsoever ye shall ask in prayer, believing, ye shall receive.' "—*Gospel Workers*, p. 263. "Not by might, nor by power, but by my spirit, saith the Lord of hosts." Zecharaiah 4:6.

A Memorial of Faith

Nyasaland, now called Malawi, is a beautiful country. It has often been called the Switzerland of Africa. Its rugged mountainous terrain, rich soil, and abundant rainfall make it one of the most picturesque parts of all Africa. Located southwest of Lake Nyasa is the Ncheu district. This district is in the Shire Highlands. The people of this area are rugged and energetic and far less vulnerable to the illnesses that plague the people living in the lowlands.

In the 1930s we had no established work in the central section of the country. The union committee voted during one of the annual sessions that Elder W. L. Davy, two African pastors, two young teachers, and I should go to Ncheu and visit the Paramount Chief with the idea that we would open mission work in that area.

Gomani, the chief, was one of the most powerful chiefs in the country. We knew that if we expected to have success and gain permission to start mission work, we would have to win Chief Gomani's friendship and good will.

We loaded the mission truck with everything we might need for our visit to the Ncheu district—food, bedding, cots, gasoline, oil, and extra springs for the truck, because this would be a long, arduous journey.

We started out. There were times when we barely crept along the rugged track. We arrived at Chief Gomani's village on a Monday afternoon. An aide met us at the entrance to the chief's village. We explained who we were and asked to have an interview with the chief.

After some delay we were ushered into Gomani's presence. The chief looked us over very thoroughly and then, turning to me, asked if he had not seen me before.

I told him that I had passed through his village some years before and had stopped to greet him.

The chief clapped his hands and smiled broadly. "Ah, yes," he said, "you dropped a gold sovereign into my hand when you said good-bye."

I nodded, but I had never expected him to remember the incident.

We explained that we had come from Malamulo Training Institute and would like to camp on the lake shore near the village.

The chief announced that he had recently completed a guesthouse, or rondavel. It had a cement floor and a Dutch-thatch roof. The chief seemed very proud of this rondavel. He added that he would be very happy to have us "christen" it by occupying it.

We thanked him for his generosity and gave him generous gifts of salt and jam and other goods.

He in turn called several young girls and ordered them to go to the lake and fetch several pots of water for us. He also ordered them to bring us firewood and some vegetables.

After unloading our camp cots, tables, food, and other equipment and putting everything in order, Elder Davy, the pastors, teachers, and I sat down to outline our plan of procedure. Then we knelt and asked God to be with us and guide us.

The next day we spent most of the time with the chief and his councilmen. We lavishly praised the beautiful district in which Chief Gomani ruled. We also complimented him on his well-run village.

We had learned during our stay in Africa that one does not rush into anything. So ten days passed before we approached the chief with our request to open mission work in the district.

When we made the request, he sat silent for a moment and then told us he would have to talk it over with his council. The very next day he informed us he had discussed the request with his council and the answer was No.

We felt very depressed, for we knew that in that tribe's entire history no decision once made had ever been reversed. We had reached the end of our human resources. But we knew that man's extremity is God's opportunity. We knew that "prayer moves the arm of Omnipotence. He who marshals the stars in order in the heavens, whose word controls the waves of the great deep, the same infinite Creator will work in behalf of His people if they call upon Him in faith." We read this statement over and over from *Testimonies*, volume 5, page 453. Then we knelt for a season of prayer.

As we rose from our knees, we all felt impressed to stay another week. During that time our teachers taught several songs to the village boys and girls. So interested were they in the songs they had learned, we decided to put on a special program for the chief. We requested him to have his throne moved out under some large shade trees while we honored him before an assembly of his people.

Before the special day arrived, we workers spent much time in prayer. On the appointed day a large crowd gathered and watched the chief ascend his throne. First of all we had the village children sing a number of songs they had learned well. The chief and his councilmen seemed pleased with the singing and performing. Knowing how much these people enjoy a good prank, we had planned several.

The chief laughed and clapped his hands in surprise and wonder. Then he called the heir to his throne and asked us to play some tricks on him. We blindfolded the young man and helped him onto a plank about six feet long and fourteen inches wide. He grasped the shoulders of two men, one standing on each side of the heir. Slowly we lifted the board off the ground while the men on either side the young man crouched.

"Be careful," one of the pastors called out. "Don't hit his head on that tree limb."

Actually he was only about four inches off the ground. But he gripped the shoulders of the two men on either side and appeared quite frightened.

"Jump!" we commanded.

But he refused to jump.

"If you do not jump, we'll have to drop you," one of the men holding an end of the plank said.

The young man seemed quite shaken, but he leaped from the board. This caused a great deal of merriment among the chief and the councilmen. The people standing around laughed loud and long.

The chief then called to me and asked me to do the trick on one of his counselors, the chief councilman. He had gone to get a drink during the past performance and had not witnessed it. I knew the man was about eighty years old, and I hesitated to play such a trick on him.

"Chief," I said, "I can't do this to him; he is old enough to be my grandfather."

"I am the chief," Gomani said. "Who are you to say No to me?"

We knew the results of gaining disfavor in the chief's eyes. We had to comply.

When the old councilman was brought forward and we blindfolded him, he trembled as we helped him onto the board and told him we were taking him for a ride in the air.

To us it seemed pitiful to watch this old man, but the chief gleefully clapped his hands and ordered us to proceed.

When we ordered the man to jump, he pleaded for mercy. But the old chief got up from his seat and shouted, "Jump!"

The old man with a great deal of hesitation and trembling finally jumped. When the blindfold had been removed, he too laughed and seemed very proud of himself.

The program having ended, it was time for us to thank the chief for his kindness in allowing us the fine accommodations, the firewood, the water, and the vegetables. We assured him that we had enjoyed our stay in the beautiful lake and mountain region. Then I added, "Chief, it has been a perfect vacation except for one thing."

"What is that?" Chief Gomani asked.

I explained that we had hoped to obtain permission to commence mission work in his beautiful, progressive area. I said no more but took his hand and squeezed it in a friendly gesture. We workers then went to the guesthouse and had another earnest season of prayer, after which we began to pack our things.

While placing some of our things in the truck, we noticed the chief and his councilmen were going into the Council Chamber. Deliberately then we began to take our time in packing away our stuff. But how long can one take to stow away one's stuff in a truck? Everything had been packed. Everything was in the truck. Everything had been tied down securely. The chief and his councilmen had not come out of the Council Chamber, and we were not about to leave.

We measured the gas and checked the oil. We checked the air in the tires, including the spare tire. The men were still in session. Although it was a hot day, I started the engine and purposefully made it roar.

Suddenly Elder Davy shouted, "Look, the chief messenger is running, waving his hands and shouting.

The man reached us and announced breathlessly, "The chief wants you to delay your departure for a few minutes."

Now we saw the chief and the rest of his councilmen walking slowly toward us. We waited, praying silently.

"Bwana," the chief said upon reaching us, "a very strange thing has happened to our tribe today."

"Chief," I answered, raising my hand, "don't be ashamed. While you were meeting, we were praying to the Great Chief of heaven who rules over all the world."

Gomani looked at us in surprise.

In faith we told him that this Great Chief whom we served had put it into the hearts of his councilmen to reverse their decision and grant our request so that they might hear the good news of the gospel. Then, exercising even more faith, we asked if the tribe would be so kind as to allow the chief guide to show us the very best available location for the new mission.

Gomani called for the guide. He was an old man in

his eighties. Where would this man lead us? Surely he could not walk far. The mission would be located nearby.

"I will respect this man's age," I informed Gomani. "I will not insist he walk too far."

Gomani looked very serious. "He will kill all of you," he said.

We did not understand this, but God had led us thus far. We would follow. So we trekked behind the guide. The first day we went several miles. I was visibly tired after traveling over the rough, hilly ground; but our energetic guide helped the other Africans and our cook prepare our tents and bed for the night.

After everything had been readied for our comfort, the guide came to us and asked permission to go with the others on a hunting trip.

It was then I knew what the chief meant when he had said, "He will kill you!"

The following day the guide led us to a site well shaded with large trees on a hilltop and in full view of the lake but not far from the main road.

The man stopped and spread his hands wide, signifying that this would be our location for the new mission. We were more than pleased to stake our desired boundary on this choice property. But the story did not end here.

Upon our return to Gomani's village he stamped his approval on our application, then forwarded it to the Government District Council. The council, made up of Englishmen, the District Commissioner, certain planters, and missionaries living in the district, sat and discussed our application. Several members of the council, led by a certain mission society, were influenced to turn down our request. We were subsequently notified of their decision.

During the session we mission workers had been reading passages from the spirit of prophecy and had been seeking the Lord in prayer. We read over and over this passage: "God will do marvelous things for those who trust in Him. . . . He will help His believing children in every emergency if they will place their entire confidence in him and implicitly obey Him."—*Testimonies,* vol. 4, p. 163.

Word came to us of the council's decision while we were in a prayer group. Immediately we called the Governor's office and made an appointment to see him. When Elder Sparrow and I arrived for the appointment, we were informed that the Governor and his wife were absent and the aides did not know where he was nor when he would return. This baffled us, but after waiting for some time we decided to start on our journey home. We could not understand what had happened. The seventy-mile journey home seemed endless. However, before the journey had been completed we found the Governor's car stalled on the road. We knew it at once by the small flag that fluttered as an emblem. There in front of the car stood His Excellency and his wife.

We stopped and introduced ourselves.

Immediately, after learning who we were, the Governor began to apologize for not keeping his appointment, but he said they had been stalled for some time. "Could I take care of the business you have with me right here?" he asked.

Knowing some of the intricacies of the mechanics of cars, I suggested that I look at the motor and see if I could fix it. I suggested that Elder Sparrow talk to the Governor while I repaired the car if possible.

Very methodically I worked. While I worked, I listened to the conversation between Elder Sparrow and the Governor. I heard the Governor ask, "Do you mean to say that Chief Gomani has approved the site the guide helped you stake out?"

Elder Sparrow assured him that that was true.

Without hesitation the Governor spoke up. "If I were you, I would plan as if final approval were already in hand. Leave the details of working it out to me."

I tightened the last bolt and announced, "You car is ready, Sir."

"That is coincidental," the Governor exclaimed. "We have just finished our conversation here."

Elder Sparrow and I thanked His Excellency, and he and his wife drove off while Elder Sparrow and I drove on our way praising God for His continued leading.

The new mission became known as the Lake View Mission. With the mission established we desired to open both an elementary and a secondary school. To open the schools we had to make application through the same Government District Committee that had at first refused our request for a mission site. However, I wrote to the District Commissioner, asking permission to sit with the official body when the application would be considered.

The request was granted. On the date set Elder Lyndon Tarr and I drove to the appointment. We were informed that I had the appointment to sit with the committee, but Elder Tarr could come in provided he did not vote.

There was an application for a mission school to be established by another mission society. This society had been well established in the area for years. We learned that its application requested the same location that we had staked out. No one spoke up. At last I stood up and moved that the application be granted.

Why did I do this? Elder Tarr had brought the book containing government rules and regulations and had handed it to me opened at the page which states that there may be more than one school operated by different organizations providing that the number of children was sufficient. We had previously counted all the boys and girls and had a list of their names and ages. When our application came up for consideration, the men began to talk among themselves, and it seemed they expected we would withdraw our request. Since no one arose to move that we be granted permission for our school, I got up again. I apologized for making all the motions, but I did move that permission be granted for the Seventh-day Adventists to begin a mission school.

There was silence for a moment. In spite of the government rule I had read, our request was refused. However, the request to open a secondary school was granted.

When a draft copy of the minutes arrived at Malamulo Mission, we called on the Director of Education for the government and explained our problem. He became indignant with the report and announced that as of that minute our school was approved.

Another gem from Sister White's writing came to mind: "Whatsoever is to be done at His command may be accomplished in His strength."—*Christ's Object Lessons*, p. 333.

Another dilemma soon faced us. Because so much time had elapsed since we had first started to work on permits for the schools and there had been so many problems standing in the way, the mission brethren had transferred the funds for schools at the Lake View Mission to another project. Now there was no money. What should we do?

The Lord does not always allow us to see the end from the beginning. If we could see the end results before we start, there would be no faith required of us. God opens the way after we take the first step, as He did with Moses at the Red Sea.

"It is impossible to separate faith from victory."

"Faith is the victory. It is not that faith gives us the victory, or helps us to win it. But faith *is* the victory."

"God's way results in certain victory for everyone."

"The accomplishments, the victories, the rewards, which compass the path of faith transcend the most captivating dreams the human imagination can comprehend. . . . Faith extends afar the horizons of human conception, and allows no limit to fence in the achievements of the heroes of belief in the promises of an infinite God."—*Without Doubt,* pp. 170, 171, 175, 176.

Once more the union committee met to study the plan and to pray about the situation. We needed money. We needed it right away. The exact sum we needed was $4000 to start the building project at Lake View Mission.

In a few days we received the exact amount of money needed—$4000. A physician in Puerto Rico whom we had never met wrote that in the night he had awakened and been strangely impressed to send $4000 to the Malamulo Mission for some special project.

The doctor said that if we did not need the money we should return it. "But if you need it," he went on, "then feel free to use it to God's glory."

Once again faith had brought victory.

We must remember that "all His biddings are enablings." The Lake View Mission, begun through faith, is carrying on a strong work today. It is truly a memorial of faith.

Success in Selukwe

After eleven years at the Malamulo Training Institute, now known as Malamulo College, Mrs. Nash and I were transferred to the Rhodesian Mission Field. There I served as president. One phase of the work I had no experience in, and dreaded, was Ingathering. The thought of it petrified me. I even went so far as to ask the union conference president if I would have to solicit in the campaign. He assured me that I would not.

When time came for the campaign to open, I felt impelled to go out and see how it was done. Of course I would go with a seasoned Ingatherer.

The first day of the campaign, Brother Searle and I went to some gold mines between Selukwe and Gwelo. Selukwe, approximately a hundred miles east northeast of Bulawayo, is in a rich mining, ranching, and agricultural district.

Along toward evening I noticed that Brother Searle seemed to be in pain. On the way home we stopped at the Gwelo Hospital. After an examination the doctor informed us that he had acute appendicitis. That meant no more Ingathering that year for my friend.

I hurried to a telephone booth and called long distance to the workers in the union office, informing them that we were in trouble and asking if they could send a replacement for Brother Searle. Immediately the union president informed me that I would have to carry on alone.

To me that seemed impossible. I could not go out Ingathering alone. That night I tried to read, but I could not concentrate. After going to bed, sleep eluded me. I rolled and tumbled and tossed until two in the morning. At last I got out of bed and fell to my knees. I asked God earnestly to give me faith in His promises. After prayer I took my Bible and opened it to 1 Samuel 10:6. This is what I read: "Thou . . . shalt be turned into another man."

Our God is a living God. His promises are living promises. By faith I claimed the promise that this text contained. Immediately the fear and burden of Ingathering rolled from me. I went back to bed and slept soundly. I arose the next morning full of faith and courage and drove back to Selukwe.

My first stop was at Meikle's Department Store. There I told the manager that the year before Meikle's had given $5 to us at Ingathering time, but this year, because of the expansion of our mission work, we hoped that the donation would be increased to $75.

Without hesitation, I was given the $75.

Next door to the department store stood the hotel, owned and operated by the same company. I told the manager there that we could not ask for a donation again, but suggested that perhaps they might be willing to give me free room and board while I was doing the Ingathering there. The manager smiled and said, "Of course, Mr. Nash. Free on the house." He assigned me to room 6.

After entering the room I fell on my knees and thanked the Lord that He had changed me into another man. While I meditated on the events of that day, the Ingathering goal that the brethren had set seemed very small. I read and thought through statements pertaining to faith, such as the following:

"It is not the capabilities you now possess or even will have that will give you success. It is that which the Lord can do for you. We need to have far less confidence in what man can do and far more confidence in what God can do for every believing soul. He longs to have you reach after Him in faith. He longs to have you expect great things from Him."—*Christ's Object Lessons,* p. 146.

"There is to be no despondency in connection with God's service. The faith of the consecrated worker is to stand every test brought upon it. God is able and willing to bestow upon his servants all the strength they need, and to give them the wisdom that their varied necessities demand. He will more than fulfil the highest expectations of those who put their trust in Him.

"Jesus does not call on us to follow Him, and then forsake us. If we surrender our lives to His service, we can never be placed in a situation for which God has not made provision. Whatever may be our situation, we have a Guide to direct our way; whatever our perplexities, we have a sure Counselor."—*Gospel Workers,* pp. 262, 263.

After I prayed for increased faith, the Lord and I increased the goal by 100 percent. And for three years I returned to Selukwe to solicit for Ingathering funds. Each year the amount collected doubled that of the previous year. God had kept His promise, and truly I had been changed into another man.

Triumphs of Faith

Bulawayo, Southern Rhodesia (now Zimbabwe), an important railroad center and trade headquarters for a vast grazing area and also a gold- and coal-mining district, had a population in the late 1930s of approximately 200,000.

Soon after the Selukwe experience I met with the members of the Bulawayo English Church and suggested that they set an Ingathering goal of $5000. The local elder felt the members could never reach that goal. He encouraged the members to vote against the increased goal.

"It can't be done," he insisted. "Now, what have you to say?"

I had been reading the book *Gospel Workers,* and the following statement flashed into my mind:

"The voice of God speaks clearly, Go forward. Let us obey the command, even though our sight cannot penetrate the darkness. The obstacles that hinder our progress will never disappear before a halting, doubting spirit. Those who defer obedience till every uncertainty disappears, and there remains no risk of failure or defeat, will never obey. Faith looks beyond the difficulties, and lays hold of the unseen, even Omnipotence, therefore it cannot be baffled."—Page 262.

With faith and confidence in the Lord, I challenged them to go out and raise the $5000. I promised that if they would raise that amount, I would add another $5000. I promised that I would not approach anyone on their donors list.

The local elder looked at me in surprise. "You don't mean what you say," he replied. "That's impossible."

I smiled at him. "Well, we'll see."

The local church members collected their $5000, but my collections came in slowly. I had to wait until someone turned the church member solicitor down. Then I would go to that person and try to collect a donation. When one man asked me how many times a year we collected and told me that someone had been to see him the day before, I had an answer ready.

"Now wait a minute," I said. "I checked the list, and your name was not on it. How much did you give?"

When he answered that he hadn't given anything, I replied, "Thank the Lord! I am glad I met you, because I prayed earnestly before coming in that you would give $75." Then I proceeded with my solicitation. At the end of our talk I invited the gentleman to kneel and have prayer with me. Upon rising from his knees, the man wrote out a check for $75 and handed it to me.

Remembering a wealthy man I had met in the city of Salisbury, a man whom I had never contacted, I decided to make an appointment and ask him for a donation. He had three secretaries, and I could not get past the first one.

I went to the telephone and called the union conference office in Bulawayo, 240 miles away, and requested them to send the gentleman in Salisbury a reply-paid telegram, suggesting an early appointment. Since he couldn't argue with a telegram, he wired back a reply Yes. The union office then called me to tell me the time of the appointment.

After the usual preliminaries when we met, I told him the reason for my coming. He replied that if he had known why I had wanted to see him he would never have given me an appointment. In turn I told him I was certain that what he said was true. I went on to tell him the steps I had taken in order to meet him.

"Well, seeing that you are here," he said, "I will give you a donation of $250."

"I cannot accept the money at this juncture," I said. "I have prayed earnestly that you would give me $3000; therefore, it would dishonor my faith if I should accept the $250."

Immediately he began to explain that he did not give away money like that. He suggested that I look over his records for the past ten years. The largest donation he had given to his own church, the Lutheran Church, was $250. "Now what do you think?" he asked as he appeared to be terminating our visit.

"Since you have asked me the question, I answer by saying I am afraid to tell you what I think because I don't want to make you angry," I replied with a smile.

"Go ahead," he invited.

"Will you promise that you will not be indignant with me?" I asked.

"No, I won't," he replied.

I paused for a moment and looked him right in the eye. Then I said, "You are not as liberal with the Lord as He has been with you."

He shrugged. "Well, it's my money. I can do with it as I please."

"But," I said, "it was through the Lord's blessing that you have what you have, and if the Lord should remove His blessing, you would find yourself in a sad condition."

He turned from me. "Well, $250. Take it or leave it."

Once more I pleaded, "Sir, I cannot accept that amount for the time being. Be kind enough to give me a few more minutes to say what I would like to say to you; then we will kneel in prayer, and I'll leave the decision up to you. You and the Lord can decide."

"That's fine," he replied and once more gave me his attention.

I made my appeal. We had prayer together. Then I removed from my pocket an addressed envelope and handed it to him. "Take this envelope addressed to me home with you. You and the Lord can decide what to do. Now don't go ahead of the Lord," I urged. "You and He decide together. If the two of you decide on only $1, that's all right. If you decide on $250, that's all right also. But you and the Lord should decide on it together." I paused and then added, "Remember the text in the Good Book that says, 'God loveth a cheerful giver.' Don't give your offering grudgingly but with a cheerful heart so that you can get the full blessing that God has in store for you."

With that I bade him good-bye.

Two days later I received the envelope at the post office. I tore it open, and out dropped a check for $3000. I rushed over to the man's office. He told me that the Lord had been harder on him than I had been. He said, "I could not sleep. I finally got up at two o'clock in the morning and wrote the check for $3000. Then I returned to my bed and immediately fell asleep."

Truly, faith in God's power is the secret of victory. "Not because we see or feel that God hears us are we to believe. We are to trust in His promises. When we come to Him in faith, every petition enters the heart of God. When we ask for His blessing, we should believe that we receive it, and thank Him that we *have* received it. Then we are to go about our duties, assured that the blessing will be realized when we need it most."—*The Desire of Ages,* p. 200.

God will do for us exceedingly abundantly, according to the riches of His glory, and the working of His mighty power. See Ephesians 3:20.

"Commit everything unto the Lord. Trust Him to help you do it and He will." Psalm 37:5, The Living Bible, Paraphrased.

"He will honor all our drafts if we will grasp His promise by living faith, and put our trust in Him."—*Selected Messages,* bk. 1, p. 300.

With God's special blessing I was able to go back to the Bulawayo Church and turn in $5000 just one week after that church had reached its increased goal.

Defeat Turned Into Victory

During the time I served as lay activities director of the Altantic Union Conference, I visited the Buffalo, New York, Church to assist with the Ingathering campaign.

The pastor and I worked all one morning but collected only fifteen dollars. Something extraordinary had to be done. We called all the church members together for a special meeting to promote the campaign and to strengthen and encourage the people. I was to take charge of the meeting. What could I say to inspire them, when the pastor and I had collected only fifteen dollars? My mind was in a whirl; the people were already assembling. I wished the floor would open and swallow me up. The song service started, and I was still wondering what I would say. I sat on the front seat and prayed earnestly while the song service continued.

At last the pastor introduced me, and I had to get up, but I still did not know what to say. I stood there, smiling at the members, but I had no message.

Suddenly a passage from *Gospel Workers*, page 262, flashed into my mind. "Faith is the clasping of the hand of Christ in every emergency." My mind began to work. When circumstances distress us and we do not know which way to turn, we can clasp Christ's hand and trust in Him. When the way is dark before us and all seems lost, in faith we can clasp Christ's hand, and He will lead us out of darkness. When we come to the end of our visible resources, we can clasp Christ's hand, and He will supply our needs. God did answer my prayer. He gave me the message that was "meat in due season," not only for the members assembled but for myself as well.

I then explained in detail to the members all about our failure of the morning. Then I added, "At first I could not understand why we were doing so poorly. But God has made it plain. He has something bigger and better in mind."

I looked at the pastor. He was leaning forward and listening most intently. I then began to explain that he and I were going to city hall to visit the mayor. "We plan to get permission to have a Tag Day—a day when the members will wear an appropriate identification and collect money from the people on the street."

Everyone knew that the church had tried to obtain such a permit for years. Never had the permit been granted. The pastor now arose and whispered in my ear that this plan would be impossible, as the mayor of the city was a Catholic and unsympathetic to Seventh-day Adventists.

Realizing that the church members were wondering what was going on, I decided to preach a sermon on faith. Afterward I turned to the pastor and asked him if he had faith enough to accompany me to the city hall.

"Yes," he replied.

I then turned back to the congregation and asked them if they had faith enough to pray for us.

They all assured us they did.

We asked them to remain in the church and in prayer while we went to visit the mayor.

Fortunately the mayor was in his office. We were ushered in and explained the purpose of our visit.

He became very agitated. "How many times do I have to say No before you Adventists understand?" he asked.

With a smile, I replied, "I suppose until you say Yes."

"Well, if you don't believe me," the mayor answered, "then take your appeal to the city council."

"When is the next meeting?" I asked.

"Tonight!" the mayor told us.

We hurried back to the church, reported how God was leading, and asked the members to continue praying.

That evening the pastor and I were present when the city council members arrived. The mayor brought up the first item of business—our request. He told the members what he had said and what we had said. Then he continued, "Gentlemen, I thought the best thing to do was to let these men hear you say No and then maybe they will understand."

I felt impressed to reply. I stood up and with a smile said, "Gentlemen, that is the strangest introduction I have ever heard. If I were not Irish—the same as your honorable mayor—I would be frightened. However, we Irish—you see, I am one-half Irish and one-half Scotch—do not think or express ourselves as other people do. Now, in modern parlance, your honorable mayor was actually saying, 'Gentlemen, I have explained the request to the best of my ability. If any of you have questions, please feel free to ask them; otherwise, vote the request up or down according to your best judgment.'"

Then I turned to the mayor and said, "Were you using an iron fist and ordering them to vote No?"

He was a heavyset man, weighing approximately two hundred fifty pounds. His florid cheeks seemed to quiver as he stuttered, "No, oh—ah, No!"

The council members clapped and clapped.

After making a few appropriate remarks we gave our appeal. The council, including the mayor, then gave us a unanimous Yes vote for our Tag Day.

The pastor and I hastened back to the church, where the members were still gathered and in prayer. We explained the outcome of our visit. Then we sang with feeling, "Praise God from whom all blessings flow."

We laid our plans well for the forthcoming Tag Day. We invited the best solicitors in the church and from nearby churches to help us. We told each solicitor that his or her home church would be credited for the amount each collected.

In a very short time nearly four thousand dollars was raised. God does work in mysterious ways, His wonders to perform.

"The believer's faith in God enables the Lord to do miraculous things for him and through him."—*Seventh-day Adventists Bible Dictionary,* p. 342.

"We need to hear with ears of faith the mighty Captain of the Lord's host saying, 'Go forward.' We must act, and God will not fail us. He will do His part when we in faith do ours."—*Christian Service,* p. 110.

We can win many victories for Christ if we are guided by His spirit.

"To everyone who offers himself to the Lord for service, withholding nothing, is given power for the attainment of measureless results. For these God will do great things."—*The Ministry of Healing,* p. 160.

Faith is the daring of the soul to go farther than we can see.

The Miracle at La Grange

While I was president of the Georgia-Cumberland Conference, it was decided the time had come to establish a church in La Grange, Georgia. There was not a single church member in that city.

Two of the leading evangelists were sent to La Grange to find a suitable location for our large tent. We would also need space for off-street parking. Naturally we were looking for an attractive location.

Since we are told that the medical work is the right hand of the gospel, we hoped to have more physicians from Loma Linda Medical School set up practice in the Georgia-Cumberland Conference. Therefore, the committee suggested I go to Loma Linda to contact prospective doctors.

However while at the university I received word urging me to hurry back to La Grange. The two evangelists were having trouble finding a suitable spot for the effort.

Upon my return to that city I went with the brethren to see the few places they had found available, but nothing was suitable.

Elder Fordyce Detamore and his group were to hold meetings for two weeks, and then Elder Kurtz would continue the meetings and build up a church.

Time was running out. We would have to hire professional help to secure a spot. If necessary we would even purchase the property. Advertising copy concerning the meetings had to be in the hands of the printer within the next four days. Elder Detamore's group would arrive and be on the payroll whether we used their services or not.

At last we went to the office of Mr. Harrison Preston, a well-known broker in the city. He agreed to show us everything he knew to be available. However, nothing he showed us met our requirements. As we were returning to his office one afternoon, we noticed a large vacant city block with only one small portion of it occupied. The lot, shaded with oak trees, was on a good street, ideal for our meetings. It would also be an attractive site for our future church.

We requested Mr. Preston to stop and let us look at the land.

"That lot belongs to the United States Government in Washington, D.C., and it is not for sale," he told us.

Back in his office he apologized that he could not help us find a suitable location, but I insisted that he had already helped us find one.

"Where?" he asked in surprise.

When I told him we wanted the property that he had told us belonged to the government, he said, "Mr. Nash, don't you understand? We cannot purchase that lot from the government in four days, four weeks, four months, or ever. Don't you know anything about government red tape?"

"Yes," I replied, "I know all about government red tape. But I also know about God's power."

The following quotation flashed into my mind. "True success in any line of work is not the result of chance. . . . It is the outworking of God's providences, the reward of faith and perseverance. . . . God gives opportunities; success depends upon the use made of them."—*Prophets and Kings,* p. 486.

In this situation I felt God was giving us the opportunity to manifest our faith in His power. I knew well the sentence from *Gospel Workers,* page 19, that says, "Workers for Christ are never to think, much less to speak of failure in their work." And it was Jesus himself who said, "If thou canst believe, all things are possible to him that believeth." Mark 9:23. Faith is the force of life.

Right then and there we asked Mr. Preston if we could kneel in his office and ask God to give us that site in four days. He agreed, perhaps a little skeptically, but we all knelt there in his office and prayed that if it were God's will and for His glory, to work it out for us so that we could purchase that piece of property.

"Now, how much should we offer the government?" I asked when we arose from prayer.

"Any amount," he said. "If God is in it, the price doesn't matter. If He is not, you won't get the land at any price."

We did not want to go too high. We offered $7500.

"That's fine," Mr. Preston agreed.

We told Mr. Preston that we would be willing to go as high as $10,000 or even $12,000.

"I think that $7500 is all right," he assured us.

He arose and went to the door to open it for us. We shook hands, and I said, "We'll expect you in our office in four days' time with good news. That will be Thursday at four o'clock.

"Yes, if we have any good news," he answered.

"Please bring the deed with you," I said. "We will present you with the check and take over the deed."

Later Mr. Preston told me that he went back into his office when we had left and sat down and stared at the blank wall, wondering if all Seventh-day Adventists were as crazy as the three that had just left him. While he was sitting there his telephone rang.

Mr. Preston told us later that that phone call had been from his brother in Washington, D.C., advising him that he and Mr. Sam Rayburn, the Speaker of the House, were leaving by plane for Atlanta, where Mr. Rayburn planned to hold a political rally. The brother had insisted that Harrison Preston be on the platform with Mr. Rayburn and himself.

Mr. Preston called his wife and told her to get ready to go with him to Atlanta. They arrived when the rally was in full swing and were ushered up onto the platform.

After Mr. Rayburn's speech he slapped everyone on the shoulder and shook hands. Coming to Mr. Harrison Preston, he grabbed his hand and asked, "What can I do for you?"

Mr. Preston replied, "Well, there is one thing, but—"

"Well, what is it?" Mr. Rayburn insisted.

"I have a client who wants something that is impossible, and I don't want to worry you with it."

Mr. Rayburn answered, "Nothing is impossible."

Mr. Preston then told him of our request for the site of land in La Grange.

Mr. Rayburn said little but left for Washington.

I do not know what happened in Washington. But this I do know. Four days later at four o'clock in the afternoon, Mr. Preston came to our office. We welcomed him and invited him to take a seat. He immediately handed me a check for $5000.

"But—but—" I stammered. "What is this for? We are buying, not selling."

"Another client wants to give us $5000 for our bargain," he said.

"We cannot accept the check," I said. "We asked God to give us the lot for His work and for a special purpose.

Mr. Preston handed over the deed to the land. Everything had been completed—in four short days—in spite of government red tape. That truly was a miracle.

"Through cooperation with Christ they [those who consecrate soul, body, and spirit to God] are complete in Him, and in their human weakness they are enabled to do the deeds of Omnipotence."—*The Desire of Ages*, p. 827.

Mr. Preston told everybody he met, including fellow club members, all about what had happened. This free publicity, with reference to the prayer and the miracle that followed, resulted in a tremendous interest in our meetings.

On opening night the huge tent was filled to overflowing. Many, unable to find seats, remained outside in their cars. The meetings were a success from the start. A congregation was raised up in La Grange and an attractive church edifice erected—all a result of the miracle.

"This is the victory that overcometh the world, even our faith." 1 John 5:4.

"All things are possible to him that believeth." Mark 9:23. Whatsoever things soever ye desire, when ye pray, believe that ye receive them, and ye shall have them." Mark 11:24.

This faith will penetrate the darkest cloud and bring rays of light and hope to the drooping, desponding soul. It is the absence of this faith and trust which brings perplexity, distressing fears, and surmisings of evil. God will do great things for His people when they put their entire trust in Him.

Through faith God's children have 'subdued kingdoms, wrought righteousness, obtained promises, stopped the mouths of lions, quenched the violence of fire, escaped the edge of the sword, out of weakness were made strong, waxed valiant in fight, turned to flight the armies of the aliens.' Hebrews 11:33, 34. And through faith we today are to reach the heights of God's purpose for us."—*Prophets and Kings*, p. 157.

FAITH

Faith is the eye that sees God,
No matter how dark the day.
Faith is the hand that holds Him
On the steep and rugged way.

Faith is the heart rejoicing—
Accepting God's promise true.
Faith is the ear that listens
To the voice that speaks to you.

Faith refuses to doubt Him,
Though others are filled with fear.
Faith is believing the Word
And knowing that God is near.
—F. M. Bates